2020

SEPARATE AND EQUAL: POEMS IN A CHANGING AMERICA

BY
CHRISTOPHER KENT

Be Not Afeard
PUBLISHING

ISBN: 978-1-7354600-1-7
ISBN: 978-1-7354600-0-0

Instagram: i.exist.for.us.to.write

BE NOT AFEARD PUBLISHING was founded in 2020
by Christopher Kent and is based out of New Hope, MN.
Cover Design by RAVASTRA DESIGN STUDIO

DEDICATION

This book is dedicated to all who felt the heartbreak
and the loss during a most challenging year.
You are not alone. We fight together.

Thank you to all who helped give my verses shape.
It means a lot.

CONTENTS

Author's Note

When I started this project, it was a direct response to Covid-19 and the uneasiness I felt. My aim was to create a body of work that could help me process the immense amount of change, while stretching creative muscles I hadn't accessed in a long time. I never thought I'd write a book.

Poetry has always existed as a tool for self-reflection but has never been at the forefront of my life. When quarantine began in March, all my theatrical projects were abruptly halted and all I had left was my day job. At the time, I was wrapping up my journey toward student teaching, and then, over the course of a week, everything was put on indefinite hold.

In this space of silence, I started to write and share my work on social media, something I hadn't even considered before. But as I familiarized myself with the platform, I started connecting with folks from around the world. I increased my appetite for poetry simply by immersing myself in a culture of writers and slowly, I gained confidence in my own abilities and voice. It felt intentional, like it was what I was meant to be doing.

And then my sister-in-law, Brianne, died. It wasn't linked to Covid-19, she simply went into a coma and never woke up. She was 27. This crushed my brother-in-law, Grant, and a week after visiting us, he was gone too. He was 34. Restrictions made funerals impossible and writing provided the grounds to work through my loss.

Shortly after, George Floyd was shot and the world, still reeling from Covid-19, was rocked again and my city of Minneapolis rose in protest. I began examining all the overlooked privileges of my life and trying to reeducate and reevaluate the toxic routines and subconscious prejudices built into my being. I didn't know what to do – but I had to do something. I had to fight back.

Again, I fell to my poems. I focused on the facts and the experiences of those with different lifestyles and challenges. I read books from different perspectives and listened to the news. I made it my mission to inform; it wasn't my conversation to lead, but I thought this would be a way to support the oppressed as an ally for change.

This book is a time capsule of my journey through this challenging and unfamiliar territory but more than that, it is a look at one person's experience in a herd of billions. The dates have been included to give a sense of the shifts in perspective and priority during this tumultuous time in our history. This book is about finding unity in the chaos that threatens to tear us apart. We are all in this together. We can be the change we need to move forward and create a world where everyone feels loved and respected. A place where we can create something worth sharing. It's not about me. We are the story. I am only a pen.

Act One:

SEPARATE

United We Wait
3.17.20

United we wait;
scared to contemplate
the next set of actions
that will inevitably reshape
the horizon of our lives.

Separated we buzz
Zoom connections
but the cut-out boxes
only temporarily
fill the desire
to create and redesign.

The uncertainty is agony,
but it's a step
in the right direction,
leading our feet to a land
modeled on newfound equality.

We exist in the face of a storm
we can't see but need
to shine our lighthouse perspective
of middle-class poverty
from sea to shining sea.

As priorities realign
we find the time
to finally breathe, rest,
and exchange the required dream
of financial stability
to pursue endeavors left
on the back burner.

Maybe now we can help the world
contained in our tiny screens,
and find the common ground
to create a vaccine for this deadly disease.

Used
3.24.20

I drive by a graveyard
of aging headstones
longing to be ferried
to the ghostly whispers
peacefully buried
beneath the quiet earth.

I pass a junkyard
of forgotten relics
riddled with age
and spot a pickup truck
mutilated with decay,
surrounded by Nature
it fought to evade.

A den of wild vines
sprawl lazily through
the cracked glass
gripping the metal and chrome,
ripping at the pristine leather
and bending this instrument
of man-made precision
to its will.

I continue to move
slowly down the roadway
as the few cars I see
blur into images
of stones and beaten trucks
and I realize the pursuits
of man are destined
to be haunted
by the spirits of the past,
and the harder we try
to grasp and claim
a piece of the world,
the quicker we fade
and are returned
to the soil.

The Lion and his Son
3.25.20

Said the lion to his son,
"Someday I'll leave your side,
you will inherit the Kingdom
to serve and lead our pride."

Said the son to his father,
"Please don't think me proud,
but even when you're dead and gone,
I still won't wear the crown."

Stunned the lion stood there,
as silent as a stone,
until finally he whispered,
"Would you refuse the throne?"

The cub looked to his father
and said as plainly as he could,
"Sir, I know it is an honor
but power isn't always good.

You make all the decisions.
You say when we eat.
You say you protect us,
but you never let us speak.

You may be our leader
but your subjects are restrained
by a system long outdated
that you claim must be obeyed.

I want to make a difference.
I want to make a change.
What have you accomplished
keeping everything the same?

The king has the authority
to choose the way to lead
but is this the kind of system
our people really need?

What if we had freedom
and a place to state our minds?
Are you really too afraid
to let us govern our own lives?

What if every animal
had a right to use their voice
and the laws of the world
were all the people's choice?

Can a ruler still be right
if he rules without consent,
you say you want the best for us
but will the silent be content?

I know you are my father
and you love me to the stars,
but this kingdom we belong to
should honor who we are.

The king remained quiet
until the child was done,
then he whispered sadly,
"If only, my son."

The Devil Visits
3.26.20

Last night the devil spoke to me.
Said, "Son it's time ya left.
You've been carrying on
these parts too long,
hiding out from death.
But I'm here to tell ya boy-o,
better count your precious breaths;
you can run real wide
but you're gonna find
I'll catch up to you yet."

Now I could've gone this morning,
my tail tucked between my legs;
could've begged for cheap forgiveness,
but I ain't been one to beg.
'Stead I told that greedy devil,
"You can try with all yer might,
but it's the bullet or the bottle,
that'll lay me down goodnight.

Then I opened wide my eyes,
stared that darkness in the face,
and I ordered him to scamper,
said his time here was a waste.
He laughed as he departed,
with a vow to be back soon.
I pulled a pistol from my pillow
and fired to say, "I hope ya do."

The Hardest Part
3.26.20

"Dad, can I go to school with you?"
It's a simple question,
and just past two,
he looks to me for answers.

Can you honestly tell a toddler
about the reality of a situation
without destroying
the security of his childhood?

I can't go, "I'm sorry son,
but Daddy doesn't know
when you'll eat snack
with your friends again,

or sit on the dolphin circle,
or make colorful castles
with the rainbow sand
from the sensory table."

I can't explain to a two-year-old
the clock is ticking,
and the alarm beeping on repeat
can't be turned off.

I can't explain how badly
I want to pack his little school bag full
with Red Panda, soft blankie,
and a dinosaur or two for the road.

I can't bring myself to form the words,

"My sweet boy,
I know it's hard for you to see,
but despite what you believe,
your Dad can't change the world."

I'll Get to It
3.31.20

Lecherous it spreads
to spider-vein a foreshadowing
as – trunk-loved – we caravan
a rush-hour metropolis.
Deep the lines echo,
recalling a splintered time
when, connected, we stood
and tied taut our glass together.
Now the perspective is split,
yet forward, unperturbed
we roll, united, in the face
of a laughing crack
in the windshield.

"Normal"
4.1.20

"What are you going to do
when we return to normal?"
she asks, but the fact is,
there's no going back.

This path we tread
is a permanent
collection of stones,
paving the days
we've been ordered
to stay at home.

It reminds our hearts
of the time
our selfish lifestyle
started to fishbowl around us,
and we were left
gasping for air.

When we were told
to keep our distance
though our survival
relied on
the kindness
of strangers.

I take solace
in the term
"New Normal"
because it means
we're moving forward,

walking with an eye on the past,
and those essential workers
we hope to never again
take for granted.

Dry Hands
4.2.20

As I begin to complain
how extremely dry
the constant washing
has cracked my knuckles,
I remember the soldiers
on the front lines
protected by week-old masks
as they selflessly try
to assist those poor souls
choking and confined alone.

The old and lonely folks
shut away for the safety
of those dying to see them
before they breathe their last
and their ventilator
is given to the next victim.

So I take a breath,
clear and clean
to reassess my situation,
and as I –
yet again
reapply lotion
to my swollen,
damaged skin –
I'm thankful that I'm able
to smell the chemicals.

You're the Mountain
4.3.20

Meghan you're the mountain
that each day
I get to climb.

You're the black coffee
that keeps me anxious
but aware that I'm alive.

You're the sun
that burns a freckle
inside my sheltered heart,

and the moon
that shines to show me
the quick switch
of light to dark.

You're the car
moving me forward
that I must maintain
or else it stops

and I'm standing
lonely on the roadside
with a smoking memory
of what I lost.

You are everything
I could've hoped for
but never dreamed would be.

You're the laughter
when I'm hopeless
and the friend
I'm meant to need.

Outside Again
4.6.20

Sun blazing down,
I navigate the sidewalk,
connected to the world
in a way I haven't been
since we began quarantine.
Back when the work-week still existed
and a Saturday felt deserved.

But it's technically the weekend
and this journey to get groceries
is soundtracked by the wind
flipping my clothes.
The rest is quiet.

I hear the leaves
whistle amidst the trees,
completely unconcerned
with current events.
I listen, transfixed in the moment,
forgetting the crisis
until all that exists is this music
I never noticed before.

Suddenly I'm dancing with abandon,
the kind I typically reserve
for liquor's confidence.
And it feels incredible,
and hopeful,
and liberating.

Then I see,
less than a block away,
a family of four coming toward me.
We exchange obligatory smiles
from the safety
of our separate patches of grass,
too scared to dare step
on the same square of sidewalk.

And as they pass,
it all comes rushing back
and I'm silenced.

Salmon Season
4.7.20

Caught between current
and where I wish to be,
a fish struggling for breath
in a fisherman's net,
lost to the mesh,
unclear what's next,
but sure it's outside
the safety of the sea.

Grant's Goodbye
4.8.20

(You can't control everything)
The words echo and bounce
these hospital walls,
as I witness a parade of gurneys
travel the whitewashed halls
en route to the next emergency.

And here she sits,
(or rather lies)
completely unresponsive,
her speech imaginary,
simulated by a machine
offering only beeps and hums
in remembrance
of what once was.

(Nothing is left)
Even her steady breath
whispers foreignly
behind the life support mask.
It's hard to stay and listen
but I feel responsible
and I know my time is limited.

She's been in this state for weeks
(I'm out of hope)
and soon I must,
(I don't want to)
for her benefit
(I can't though)
and those who desperately
need the resource,
(please, no)
pull the plug,
(this sucks so much)
and let her go.

Not My Grief
4.8.20

It's not my grief
so why does it
grip my heart
this deeply?
Why do I see
a moving picture
of a defeated man
holding his wife's
lifeless hand
as she slips
forever
from his world?

His tears
are not mine
to show
but they flow
without warning
creating a fraud
of my body.

Am I trying
to write out
the loss
that I feel
by rewatching
the moment
he was forced
to turn her off?

It's not my grief,
but still I'm lost
in his thoughts.

Social Media
4.9.20

What is social media?

Is it a gathering of folks
akin to a conservatory,
where artists of various mediums
can share and expose the world
to the wacky and impassioned
aspects of their souls?

Or is it a den of egos,
desperate for validation
in an age
where merit and confidence
are hopelessly linked
to each creation they post?

Or is it both?

Said the Air
4.10.20

Out for my normal
morning drift
I find myself
amid a warzone,
a solitary specter
among the aftermath
of silent life,
the bodies spared
are tucked inside,
clinging to their machines,
afraid of me.
Afraid to die.

Two Sides
4.13.20

An argument
is comprised
of conflicting sides
where both are wrong
and neither right.

Each is well thought out
and believes the other,
without a doubt,
is widening the scar
of what's passed on.

Nobody's perfect,
we're stained with the change
we choose to admit,
swapping the facts
in search of a stronger argument.

Who are we when we're fighting to win?
Who are we when we're crumbling
in separate directions,
too lost in the lie of our pride
to see a way back to each other?

And what happens to the home
we constructed together
from the bones
of a shared dream?

Often we forget to remember
when our two sides
are connected
they're made complete.

Tiger King
4.14.20

Weeks in
and I begin to feel happy.

The stress is starting to fade,
replaced by a community

conscious of its neighbors.
The capture the flag mentality

of election season,
has switched to concern

for the children of the world
going hungry without school.

Resources are finally
being creatively mined

to benefit humanity
and provide hope.

We're all in the same boat.
The water spilling the sides

is shared, as is the care
with which it's handled.

The civil divide
ripping America in two,

is put to better use- sorting through
the shitstorm of this pandemic.

We may be floundering
under the weight of the unknown

but at least we agree on something,
even if it's only Tiger King

and the decision
to stay home.

Creation
4.16.20

is to listen
to the magnificent
expanse
of the universe
and whisper,
"Yeah,
I could add a verse."

A Reminder
4.16.20

I awake at 4:00 a.m.
and the day proceeds
in a routine blur:

I shower, shave,
and snag a banana
on my way out the door,
noticing it's underripe
as I drive like a shadow to work.

Neatly parked
in my assigned spot,
I start the trek inside,
each step echoing to remind
how many hours I give to this place.

Next I'm checked to ensure I'm healthy
and alert for the tasks of the day.

Then at last,
after all the tests,
I step into my office
and immediately receive the update:
all the beds are full.

I don my uniform
with groggy, rehearsed precision
and notice for the first time
a small sign
hanging crooked on the wall,
"I made this world shine for you."

I finish tying tight my scrubs,
double checking
my mask is well-secured.
It may be cliché,
but that line leads me with a smile
to the first patient I must serve.

In Deep
4.20.20

Deep in the gentle alcove
of your breath,
as vibrations issue
from the folds
of your vocal cords,
I discover your truth,
most elusive.

A timeless music
captures the air
and promises
to swallow
the chatter
of the world.

You speak
and I hear
the reason
for conversation.
You laugh
and I rediscover
the sound of elation
in your eyes.
I smile in the expanse
of your echo
and crave the release
of your sigh.

Isolated
4.22.20

Crowded thoughts
suffer hard
the loneliness
of quarantine
like a nervous valedictorian,
standing at the podium,
dressed to impress,
but holding
a stack
of sweat-stained cards
no one will ever see.

Covid Kid
4.24.20

"Dad, can we go to the park today?"
Five months into two
and he already knows
the definition of quarantine,
for the world's new normal
is the reality
he was only beginning to form.

He's close to identifying
the entire alphabet,
M and W are still tricky,
but that boy understands
why everyone in the store
is Wearing a Mask,
and that the house
has become a fortress
we must return to.

I wish I could explain the virus,
map out the path
of this sickness
for him to comprehend,
but how do you dad,
when the facts are elusive
and all you can do
is pretend
you're not scared, too?

"Not today, son"
is all I can afford to say.
"OK" he replies,
as his balloon deflates
and he goes back
to playing
with his garbage truck,
and it's stupid,
but I'm ashamed.

A New Desk
4.27.20

Time is absolutely
the currency to invest in,
and now,
given the state of things,
I'm flush with it.
Gigs and contracts are replaced
with building a new office space
for distance learning,
a sacred place
to delve into the self
and create meaningful work.

It's easy to slip into a mindset
focused on what I've lost,
but when I look back
on this pandemic,
It'll be nice to scan
old notebooks,
stuffed past capacity,
with scribbles spent
at the fresh desk
I built for myself.

Call me selfish,
but a testament to the time
I filled my life
with what I loved,
sounds better than agonizing
over the loss
of what I could've done.

Invisalign
4.29.20

I stare into the mirror,
taking stock of all my teeth,
making note of every movement,

every shift another reason
to correct the imperfections
few will ever see.

Subconsciously, we remain aware
of every aspect of our flaws,
cataloguing each critique

until the self-portrait
we have painted
makes us feel
inadequate to be ourselves.

Waiting
4.30.20

The poet resides
underneath
a paradise of sky,
breathing in harmony
with his calling,
awaiting the bombshell of a virus
to strip his life and purpose,
like an icicle
poised to fall
on the helpless.

Emerald Sky
5.1.20

Slowly the world
begins to return
to its usual ignorance,
the rules are left
for others to abide by,
masks kept in the closet,
forgotten like the floss
that goes unused,
even though we know it exists
right there in the cabinet.

I remember my first
cavity being filled.
I was falling from reality
to the tune of ocean waves
employed to keep me calm,
and from the window I could see
an emerald green haze
pervade the clouds,
and then the sound
of the drill broke in
and all was gone.

Now as I gaze
toward the pale green sky
swirling high above me,
I can't help wonder if its color
is a warning of another shade to come,
and like my dentist,
it's reminding me
there's more I could have done.

A Summer Adventure
5.4.20

It's the weekend,
the weather
a gorgeous glow
of warmth
inviting the mind to explore.
And here we sit,
bored and itching
for any excuse to flex
our fading youth –
So off we go, out the door
into the great expanse
of nature's growth.
Possibilities abound
as we click our belts
and hit the road
with the spit and grit
of freshly-licensed teenagers.
Sunglasses donned,
windows down, we soar,
the whipping wind
chilling our skin
but we refuse to lose
a single stroke
of the picture
we've created
for our intrepid trek
to the hardware store.

Within
5.6.20

Tightly dressed
in the embrace of night,
we lay before each other,
eyes wrapped
in silent conversation,
anticipation daring us forward.
Breath catches as time freezes
only to quickly thaw
in the skillful second
of each button freed.
Exposed and laid open,
we explore the soft spaces
behind shy clothes,
the places revealing
our unspoken truths.
In this moment of need,
we rise and fall,
a rhythm mounting,
moving toward
the sweet echo of eternity
that cries to cover us.
And in this slow
return to time,
we fade to the damp sheets
draped against our skin,
and all is still,
eyes pooling sweetly
into the depths
we discovered
while within.

I'll Remember
5.6.20
   - in memory of Brianne Berkland

I'll remember her laughter
the way she could talk,
searching for a story in every topic.

I'll remember being escorted
through the crowds of New Jersey
by a talkative tour guide -
how proud she was of her homeland.

I'll remember that late night
on the farm,
cold as balls,
and us sliding like goons
across the icy deck
like we had nothing to lose.

She lived like that,
heart open for all,
a soul for every occasion.

Grant,
I knew only an aspect
of the power she embodied,
but I know for certain
she loved you from the first
accidental rendezvous
when a drunk pedestrian
jumped before your car
and she rushed the road
with a fire in her eyes
that would forever
keep you driving
through her life.

She loved Jersey
but she found her real home
that night she took your hand
and began her joyride
as your wife.

Mi Amor
5.7.20

You're the perfect beer,
the one I scoured the shelves
in search of what I believed
could be out there.

I spent my college nights
hunting through bottles
of build-your-own six packs
looking for a memory
of a night, long ago,
when I first discovered
it could taste so good.

One summer evening
I stumbled to a bar stool,
and there you were,
your beautiful color
drew me in
and the shape of your neck
so slender,
your label
enticingly creative -
I knew I had to ask
to take a sip.

And now, years later
I only have to sample
your aroma,
to realize
the brew of you
is better than any
I will remember
because I can
sip you warm,
foam to dregs,
never getting full,
always wanting more
of that woman
I will forever call,
"Mi amor."

If Walls Could Hear
5.8.20

If walls could hear,
they'd hear a man
breathing all alone
as he stares longingly
out the window,
watching a young robin
build her cozy nest
for a family quickly coming.

If walls could hear,
they'd hear the shuffle
of routine feet
assisting the man
from the chair to bed
and back again,
and the barrage of insults
issuing from a man
exhausted from sitting this long.

If walls could hear,
they'd hear an old man
fumble with his phone,
punching in the only
number he knows,
waiting and hoping
to hear her voice.
"Maybe tonight,"
they'd hear him whisper,
but they'd know the truth,
the number's been
disconnected for three years
and it's only the dementia
keeping the old man's
love and drive alive
in this quiet nursing home.

If walls could talk
they might say,
"I'm sorry your robin's flown away,
but it's ok to let go
and fly too."

Impressive
5.10.20

Impressive –
the word I heard from all the friends
who played in the fantastic wonderland
of my childhood.

And they didn't see
the half of it.

They didn't see
the Magic School Bus books
you would save for being good.

They didn't see
you stand in line after line
to collect the gift at the top of my list.

They didn't see
us sorting mounds of Legos by color
just to spend some time together.

They didn't see
us watching Cubs' double-headers
late on a school night
because Dad was states away
learning to make beer
and you felt lonely.

They didn't see
me make a colossal mess
and run away, only to slowly
return to a forgiving hug
and the compassion found
in a "welcome home, son."

But it's true,
they're right,
you've always been the strength
that built the foundation of my life.

And mom,
it's damn impressive.

Effect of Covid-19
5.13.20

When this whole thing began,
damn, was that really March?
Honestly, it's become
too harsh on my mind
to look back
or keep track of the time.

At the start, I scoffed at the way
the plight in China was portrayed:
a new calamity created to appease
the media's constant need
to sensationalize.
Another ratings boost
that soon would fade.

As the days on the calendar
swiftly flipped at a frantic a pace,
the overall outlook changed.
People began to speculate
about the speed of the spread
from China to Italy
and how quickly
it could reach our shores.

Would we be equipped to face
a large-scale epidemic
or would we too, fall short?
When our hospital beds
fill to capacity with sick patients,
would we be ready
to answer the ill
with innovative solutions?

And then it hit home,
slowly at first,
like the minor inconvenience
of a leaky drain,
just grab a larger bucket
and hope it holds,
but the pipe was old
and it burst with the force of a wave.

I couldn't ignorantly laugh
behind my handmade mask –
this was a war
we weren't prepared for.

The nuclear threat we expected
turned out to be a disease
hidden in the air we breathe.

In the wake of this tragedy,
I felt an obligation to the world.
But what could one man do
to combat an attack
mounting every day?
What could I achieve
shut away
from the family and friends
I needed to help me believe
this wasn't the end,
and when the nation
made my time constraints
the same as they'd ever been
by naming me essential?

And then it dawned,
with everything in limbo,
I didn't have an excuse
to ignore my passions.
I could write poetry
to my heart's content
and use my words
to hug a socially distant world
and off I went,
pouring out thoughts
like rain in the grip of a storm,
throwing myself to the wind
as vulnerable as a newborn.

I found myself surrounded
by artists of all ages
digging through their veins
for the lifeblood they'd stored,
but never shown.

Now they stood confidently
upon the stage of social media
and it was beautiful.
A waterfall of creativity
came spilling from lonely homes
to those caught by the virus.

Each day more information is released,
the dead increases and we stay scared
and locked inside.

But if this is a war,
I'm among a battalion
I proudly stand beside:
a wonderful array of soldiers
of every shade and hue,
six feet apart,
ready to break through
the might of this pandemic
with the hope they hold onto.

The masks may make us muffled
but our voices clearly say,
"United we will conquer
whatever comes our way."

As I listen to this war cry,
I hear the purpose I've ignored:
all I am is the heartbeat
I earn with my words.

From the Driveway
5.14.20

Too aware of the recycled air,
you stare out the window
a mix of longing and shame
permeating the tiny space
where you've encased yourself.

Gazing toward
what you once called home
your fingers play
a melody of anxiety
on the steering wheel's
worn out leather.

Your knuckles whiten,
as the memory of you and her,
and that night
circulate
until you can't bear it any longer.

When the foundation
you built together,
crumbled.

There's nothing
left of you now
but the house-keys
dropped
on her doorstep.

You take your hands off the wheel
long enough to put it into gear
and drive away,
but remain,
too ashamed to pursue
the you that you knew,
but too scared
to leave the driveway.

Facing the Dragon
5.15.20

At first glance
a blank page
can appear
like an adversary
that must be overcome
by a masterpiece.
It may seem
like fragmented thoughts
of scribbled lines
almost crossed-out,
lack the gravitas
to be worthy
of the pure white canvas
staring like a dragon
before the sword
of your pen.

But then again,
there's no use crying
over spilled ink
for what you discover
in the endeavor
of creating
is seldom perfect,
instead you uncover
a part of yourself
beating beneath
the cruel critique
of the dragon's breath,
daring you to make
the first attack
and let the fire
inside your heart
win out at last.

I Made the Bed
5.19.20

I made the bed this morning,
pulled the sheets tight
to reach the edges,
made sure all the flowers
faced the proper direction,
laid them flat and smooth,
tucked in every crevice,
to protect your feet
from the cold of when I roll
and try to steal the blankets
as you say, like a walrus
fast asleep after a hard day.

I made the bed this morning,
hoping to fix the way
I treated you,
but as I fluff all the pillows
I said we didn't need,
it's so painfully obvious
what a mess the bed is
without you
to make it neat.

True Love
5.21.20

He holds her hand,
listening to her breath
steadily fading away
and whispers
through the gasps,
"It's ok, my love,
we had a good run,
surrender,
I'll stay."

Reopen
5.22.20

Things start to reopen and I think
at last, the normal lifestyle I lived
before all this Covid-shit
made me second guess
whether or not it was worth it
to take a walk outside,
or get a week's supply of groceries,
or get gas without wearing a mask,
or visit a friend
whose spouse just died.

But then I drive to the hospital
and wait two hours
just to check in,
unsure they know I exist
and as I sit,
alone,
I realize
how wrong I was,
things may be opening,
but the world I understood
had a major facelift
that's beyond recognition.

And I look,
and notice the Waiting Room
is full again with people
who just came in
and I must face the fact
that this is normal.

Reaching for Cherries
5.25.20

Dangling on the cusp of opportunity,
I lean through the deep expanse of leaves
hoping to grasp a tiny portion of the red cherries
waiting to be squeezed and tasted,
falling and calling inside the shadow of green,
whispering of a juice too exquisite to slip
silently into the abyss of 'if only'

No, this exquisite memory
will forever be held and remembered
as the moment I dared to be blatant
and drank the red within the leap.

Perspective
5.27.20

Raw and chapped,
my lips crack
under the ceaseless pressure
of this over-washed
and faded
handmade mask I wear
to protect and claim
a semblance of control.

But can I complain
when my doorstep
continually boasts
of essential hands
ensuring my Amazon
whim awaits?

Act Two:

EQUAL?

Minneapolis is on Fire.
5.28.20

Minneapolis is on fire.
The news flashes scenes
of protesters screaming
and throwing rocks at police.
Hundreds of enraged citizens
surround the precinct that employed
the officer responsible
for the brutal murder
of George Floyd.

I'm disgusted.

Not with the brave souls
daring infection, tear gas,
batons and rubber bullets –
No, I'm disgusted
by the history of racist violence
that still exists and persists
in every corner of the globe.
I'm disgusted
that people still harbor
a blind hatred for folks
they don't even know
and the injustice
that those most at risk
must burn down an Autozone
before we take notice.

This is not new.
Police have been killing
African Americans
with impunity for decades,
the difference is
we live in a video era
that can spread
those gut-wrenching words,
"I can't breathe. I'm about to die."
to every otherwise ignorant home.

Minneapolis is on fire
and I understand the anger
and frustration at a nation
that doesn't value the rights
of each individual in its population
and refuses to press charges
against power hungry men
exploiting their position
to prey on the defenseless.

It's like a bad movie plot
"man arrested for a potentially
counterfeit $20 bill."
It sounds even worse when you state:
Derek Chauvin, a man of the law,
knelt on the neck of
a 46-year-old George Floyd
for seven minutes
while three other officers
stood and watched,
until all that could be heard
was an onlooker's shocked,
"they just killed him."

Minneapolis is on fire,
and it's scary
because it's my home
and I don't know
what's on the horizon.
But I'm not upset
that Target was looted last night.
I'm upset
that someone lost their life
in what was supposed to be
a peaceful protest.

Is this what the city needs?
I can't say because I'm only an ally
to a larger conversation.
I'm not among those being constantly shot
and yelling for retribution
in the wake of a tragedy
that means society still isn't listening
to a community being murdered
out of fear and racial profiling.

Minneapolis is on fire
and maybe it's out of turn,
but I believe in equality,
so I say, let the fucker burn.

Privilege
5.31.20

The neighborhood is quiet
as my beat to shit Honda Fit
ghosts its course to the grocery store.
The light of the fires and riots,
blazing out of sight,
are easily ignored.

With my guilt and privileged circumstance,
I bypass the intense, winding line
to get a couple of six packs.
It seems odd the owners
aren't concerned by swarms
of booze-seeking customers,
considering the liquor stores being looted
a mere fifteen miles in the distance.

A quick selection, a swift trip
along the designated circles,
I'm out and in my vehicle,
prepared to easily exit.

Routinely I glance the rearview
and spot a couple,
African American,
right behind me.
I scold my soul
for noticing their color
and decide to speak.
So akin to my ignorance
I lower my mask,
roll down the window,
raise my fist
in what I believe is solidarity
and say, "Black lives matter."

And immediately,
without judgment or animosity,
they both reply, "Thank you."
I've never felt more white in my life.

I wonder as I resume my drive,
if privilege is a lack of impediment
to act without fear,
am I adding my voice to the protest
or only unloading
the guilt I feel?

What's Louder?
6.2.20

the reaching gasps
of trapped breath,
restrained by prejudice's
strong knee?

or the screaming wheels
of racist judgment,
careening like an executioner
toward protesters
peacefully gathered
on the highway?

or the cacophony of sound
echoing the streets,
as thousands
continue to march,
unafraid to attack
the oppression
that holds them down?

Not for the Movies
6.3.20

Real grief is not for the movies.

It is slow.

Silent.

A torrent of memories
as you remember
the smallest seconds,
now precious,
those tiny artifacts
that torture your mornings.

A birthday balloon half inflated,

an old and faded T-shirt,
hanging like a ghost
behind the bathroom door,

a blanket that still holds their shape.

This script you've saved
is not cinematic,
it defies a neat narrative
as it continues
to sporadically play
every time you close

or open your eyes.

A Hug Is
6.4.20

solidarity,
an embrace
that states, nonverbally,
"I don't understand,
how could I possibly?
But I'm here,
and though I'm armed
with the details
of your unique situation,
I can't speak
to what you're going through.
But I hope my presence,
in this moment,
serves as a small support
to lift your heart
to the next step
and away from the torment
you're entitled to feel."

It says "I'm sorry," without pity,
because it acknowledges
the sad fact of what happened,
without tacking on cliched platitudes
that never console
or bring back what was stolen.

It allows both parties
to fall into each other
and be vulnerable.
When everything else
dictates a strength
and resolve to move forward,
those arms welcome a release
and a break from thought.

It's a brief liberation
that can't be spoken,
only felt.

Leaves of Flame
6.5.20

Ash from the riots
rain from the trees
like confetti shards,
a celebration of life
burning to honor
the unforgotten,
unable to escape
the red and blue
lights of injustice,
the whispers of hatred
no longer hidden
behind a white-
washed curtain,
as we finally
book those responsible
for the crimes against
the innocent
they burnt and bled
and forced to fall
forever silent.

#Newsfeed
6.9.20

A new, sensationalized news segment
grips society with the scene
of gruesome violence
while Instagram fills
with black boxes
promoting silence.

The world bleeds for justice
under fire from police
while the media
repeats the narrative:
a "choking" Black man
now "deceased."

He was murdered.
That's the truth.
They can use fancy words
like "alleged"
to sugarcoat the facts
but the cop has been charged
with second-degree manslaughter
and George Floyd is dead.

A movement needs a platform
to amplify the message
it promotes,
but a news clip
and a quick-to-click article
doesn't mean you're informed.

A political party doesn't fit
everyone the same,
we must dig deep into a belief
before we can advocate
for change.

Don't scroll your phone
and feed your soul
with every story they endorse.
Don't accept a headline -
read past your bias
and critique the main course.

Tug-of-War
6.10.20

Two sides stand,
Red vs. Blue
across the aisle,
separated by
what justice means
to each,
aligned with pride
to the home team
they cheered beside
since birth.

Fresh-faced strangers
push and pull
in a tug-of-war
as old as the dirt
of their ancestors,
neither party
giving an inch,

fearful
of appearing weaker
than the strength
of all the others
who dug their feet
in the firm belief
this land
was theirs to win.

The Air We Breathe
6.12.20

Heartbreak
is the air we breathe,
a constant concoction
of fear without relief,
waiting to hug
the loved one
you haven't seen
outside a screen
for weeks.

A heavy dose
of disgust
pumps the lungs
as you witness
the police
you once trusted
operate
with violent hatred
and corruption.

You choke
on the ash
watching riots
blaze families
homeless
and try to atone
your compliance
by submitting
your voice
to the protest.

You scream
into the fabric
of a DIY mask,
joining a chorus
of fists
raising an attack
on the past.

24 Seasons
6.13.20

For the first time ever
a Black man
will be the next Bachelor.

Isn't that remarkable?

It took them 24 seasons
to cast a Black man
in the title role.

Now, is it a good show?

Well, I wouldn't say so,
but who am I to judge
someone looking for love?

What I think doesn't matter,
because I don't tune in,
but millions do,
and it took them
24 seasons
to put a Black man
in the spotlight.

Does that seem right to you?

Celebrating 31
6.15.20

Last night we celebrated my birthday
in the midst of a Covid world.
My wife cocooned in her recliner,
keeping the pain
of a broken clavicle at bay
with drugs that force her eyes closed.
My best friend digging
into a brutal assortment of wings,
sprawled the length of a blow-up mattress
recruited to add whimsy to the evening.
My son off to grandma's farm for a weekend,
our recent splurge of a flatscreen TV
fills the absence with loud abandon:
the long-awaited Artemis Fowl.

All was good.

But the movie was terrible,
a dumpster fire blockbuster,
that took a successful book
and determined
the best course of action
would be to throw out
everything Colfer had written.
Not the kind of nostalgia I expected
after waiting twenty years
for an adaptation.

Absolute garbage.

But I loved it
because I was home among family
who show they care by being there.

And as we retire to sleep at 9:30,
I laugh and smile,
knowing I wouldn't celebrate
any other way.

Traveling Through
6.16.20

Long road trips are the worst
for chaining back memories,
they swirl and rise, a chorus,
a symphony of skeletons
conducted by each shift
in this mundane landscape.

I hear the voices beneath
the hum of this aging motor,
a low moan that speaks
a language I once could translate
but have forgotten, almost.

These tears taste awful
as the road continues to sprawl
and paint my thoughts with questions,
the same ghosts of blame
I always face on this long,
empty highway towards home.

"Criminal"
6.17.20

"Criminal" is the word they use
to ensure communities are safe.
"Criminals" are prey from whom
they take and take and take.

I recall the blurry photographs
showcased on the evening news,
the media stereotypes created
to easily frame the men accused.

I was taught to see the shades
of brown faces as the same
as I learned of segregation
and the treatment of the slaves.

I was fed the propaganda
saying racists met defeat
by railroads made in secret
and Martin Luther's dream.

I retained nothing of the culture
but hopelessness and fear,
studying Black History
every other year.

I gobbled up the textbooks
that spun a fairytale of war
full of white knight abolitionists
who thought they evened out a score.

I read our origin like a movie,
a cinematic piece of art,
the climaxes made compelling
by a fabricated arc.

The founders of our nation
became the underdogs designed
to mask the masters of oppression
who wrote themselves to shine.

In the name of liberty and justice
we struck out from the Brits,
we sold our flag of freedom
with bold ideas from souls of grit.

I got wrapped up in the glamour
of the fight to overcome,
but never saw the country
for what it was and what we'd done.

Any person who looked different
than a white-washed male ideal
was brought up to be a patriot
but always forced to kneel.

I grew up in a castle
protected by police,
I never met injustice
for the sake of my beliefs –

or the color of my skin,
or what I chose to wear,
or where I had to live,
or a past I had to bear.

My innocent, young ignorance
made it easy to ignore
the wealthy shackles of America
that chained its people poor.

Now the books I'm reading
are penned by other sides,
from perspectives unfamiliar,
still fighting for their lives.

Each page hits like a bullet
and reveals the awful truth:
I'm a product of compliance
and there's nothing I can do

to apologize to a people
I naively thought were free
as their bodies stacked like fish
in a can of cold sardines.

All the people born to suffer
for all that's come before,
unable to mature
from behind a prison door.

Enslaved by trumped up charges
and petty little slips,
misdemeanors turned to felonies
unless you're white and rich.

I know I am responsible,
an accomplice to the crime,
no longer pleading ignorance
but sure I'll never serve the time.

I feel the guilt and shame
of all the wrongs I didn't see,
I was taught to spot a criminal
but that "criminal" is me.

Deserve
6.18.20

My sister has a wife
who's now my sister
and their wedding was painted
in all the colors of their joy.
I remember standing right beside them,
donned in vibrant, pastel orange,
and thinking,
how beautifully they complement
the other's unique soul.
It doesn't matter if I know you,
you deserve to feel the kiss
of a partner who just promised
to bear witness to the trip
the two of you will share together,
no matter what you face,
a union, born by love,
that no one has the right to take.

I Can't Pretend
6.19.20

It's odd the memories you conjure
when you fumble through a loss
of two people you were close to,
who's hearts just chose to stop.

I'm sitting on a colossal log
full of moss and sap,
a scorching campfire heats my legs,
leaves stretch to touch my back.

Our summer gig is ending,
tonight's send-off will be bright,
time for one last celebration
before we head back to real life.

The hour is fast approaching
to share the moments that we felt
the spirit move to guide us
to the campers that we helped.

I sit beneath the starlight
trying to organize my thoughts,
listening to the popping flames
as each shadow stands to talk.

In second grade, I walked the trails
and quickly found a home,
I climbed the path to counselor
but why I didn't know.

All summer I'd been searching
for a reason to go on,
teaching lessons from a textbook
full of contradicting laws.

When everyone had finished,
all eyes fell to wait my rise,
and I knew the time had come
to voice what plagued my mind.

I told them it was over,
I no longer could support
a force promoting love
of only certain sorts.

I spoke about the Bible,
said the message was sincere
but the stories it promoted
preyed on loneliness and fear.

I said I loved the people
faith had welcomed to my life
but I knew I couldn't worship
a creator named The Light.

I didn't need a cult to lead me
or some robe to hear me pray,
all I wanted was a place
to feel safe and unafraid.

I sat and cried that evening
in front of all my friends
and though they tried consoling,
I'd never see those friends again.

Next year, I called the camp
I'd attended in my youth,
but they told me it was over,
there was nothing I could do.

And when I hung the phone up,
I vowed right then and there,
I'd never seek an answer
in the fable of a prayer.

But now I sit and wonder,
as I stare before this page,
if what I ran away from
could be used today to save

the people full of laughter
who harbored hidden shame,
since I don't believe in heaven
have I laid them in their graves?

I don't have a sea of angels
to lead me to their sides,
I don't have a larger plan
to make sense of why they died.

All I have are a few pictures
of the times now come and gone.
Did I know what I was doing
when I turned my back on God?

I was raised to be a Christian,
I know the way to cleanse my sins.
I remember well the scriptures
but the words won't honor who I am.

The idea of life eternal,
would be a comfort, this is true,
but I can't pretend to have the power
to bring them back with You.

We Didn't Change – We Froze
6.20.20

Days move at the same rate.
Nothing ever slows,
no matter how you
pound the pavement,
at an office or at home,
the work leads the body
to exhaustion
until it's lying cold,
clutching hard the paper dollars
it sacrificed a heart to hold.

We didn't change – we froze.

At first assistance came in bursts
keeping us afloat,
but as the toll of the pandemic
forced businesses to close,
the government pulled support
from those unable to afford
to lose a day of work
or the means to stay at home.

We didn't change – we froze.

The real threat to choke society
isn't a virus we can't see,
it's the economy restarting
on the same route as before:
benefiting corporations
that won't provide relief
for an exhausted population
who already can't obtain
the insurance that they need
to rest and breathe.

We didn't change our greed – it only froze.

Goal
6.21.20

The parenting fear is real.
Will I be enough for him?
Will I earn the money to form
the happy playground home
that Avery deserves to grow up in?
My goal's to be the Dad
I learned to respect: the kind of guy
who killed the day at two jobs
but had enough life left at night
to inspire new Lego creations.
The bar's set high and I'm terrified
I won't measure up to the man
who fought with all the strength he had
to stay above the bullshit
pulling him down.
He never let me see a slip.
He never quit.

I was far from perfect.
The kind of kid who marks out
a treasure map
on the freshly painted walls
in permanent ink.
A late-maturing handful:
who died his hair black,
stole crap from Hot Topic,
wrecked three cars,
got kicked out of college,
and got too drunk at his sister's beauty pageant
to meet his grandma for breakfast.
Like the music I screamed
and cycled through,
he let me play it out.
If I can maintain that patience
with my own son,
I'd be worthy of his praise,
the product of calloused hands,
molded with compassion and drive,
made into a Dad by one who chose to try.

Father's Day, 2020
6.22.20

Before him
you stand,
a shaking hand
pressed firmly
against his fingers,
almost overlapping,
gripping the glass
as the distance of the window
traps this moment in tragedy
and you mouth
"hello" and "goodbye"
in one breath,
to your father,
quarantined and kept alone
inside the nursing home.

Ode to Iowa
6.23.20

A tall pile of corn, shucked and resting
in a well-constructed stack, or waiting

outside in a field of vast space, a sea
of green, waving friendly, spreading

toward the unobscured horizon,
grown for the benefit of a community,

consumed by the hungry, the culmination
of generations of experienced hands,

reliant on this year's yields,
sweating to put food on the table.

The Rockstar of America
6.24.20
   - quotes are taken directly from Donald Trump's June 20th, 2020 Tulsa Rally at the BOK Center in Tulsa, Oklahoma.

Saturday night, in Tulsa, Oklahoma,
the Rockstar of America
gathers his courage
and shuffles toward the podium.
The dark blue suit and red tie,
symbols of PR design,
are backlit by the flashing sign,
"Make America Great Again."

"We're going to build a future
of safety and opportunity
for Americans of every race,
color, religion, and creed,"
the celebrity of our country
states with rehearsed authority
into the microphone, feeding
us the poetry we wish to believe.

He proceeds to boast of the economy
and TVs in Air Force One planes
and the 212 miles of wall
that will protect against
the "very tough hombres,"
that will "break into American homes."

He defines the protests as
"extremism and destruction
and violence of the radical left."
Labels Covid-19: "Kung Flu"
and the "plague that China sent,"
blown way out of proportion by CNN.

He justifies, for 10 minutes,
why he couldn't use a ramp
without assistance,
and spends a majority of his speech
bullying a potential, presidential candidate.

He threatens the cost
of a "petroleum free" economy,
calls windmills, "bird killing machines"
moves from the "fake news"
of our environmental crisis
to the arm strength it takes to salute.

He rails, "the radical left plans
to obliterate your constitution"
and "take away your guns"
but "he will make America safe"
by "appointing more judges
to interpret the Constitution as written",
an ancient piece of parchment
created by rich white dudes
to oppress the poor.

But nothing of George Floyd,
or Breonna Taylor,
or the hundreds of others
killed by racist police,
he focuses on the financial cost
of defunding the force.

He pats his own back,
complements his staff
and stands before the mass,
unmasked, urging his audience
"not do anything stupid on November 3rd."

He wraps his act
with the signature hashtag,

"A vote for Republican is a vote
for better schools, better jobs,
safer families and stronger communities
for all Americans."

Which sounds great until you recall
the guns, the wall, the Kung Flu,
the petroleum, the bullying,
the wealthy, the fake news,
and all the other shit

he took the time to spew
without once mentioning
the meaning behind the movement
holding one statement to be true:
Black Lives Matter.

Black Lives Matter,
you arrogant, old fuck,
not that you spent two trillion
to rebuild the military,
or that the borders are secure.
Black Lives Matter.
Not Joe Biden.
Not the state of
Anderson Cooper's hair.
Black Lives Matter.

If you really wish to be
the Rockstar of America,
Mr. President,
sing something people haven't heard.
You claim to be original
but we already know the words.

New Moon
6.25.20

I swim in the recess of your soul,
like a turtle pulled by the moon,
the stretch of light you yawn
calls my world to sleep
in the calm arms
of your oceanic
worldview.

Two Birthday Trips
6.26.20

To celebrate, we collect at Kent Park
and spread the silver-lining of Covid-19
the whole length of a rotting picnic table.

Bellies full, we navigate a playground palace,
lost to our toddler's shadow, hyped to capacity,
on the sweet euphoria of grandparents.

With gymnast ease, he scales the rockwall,
while we, two breaths behind, drip worry
and sweat, down the cacophony of slides,
echoing the strength of his carefree laugh.

Detached and ready for the next adventure,
he gives chase, only to be locked for a moment
in a mother's strong and safe embrace.

He screams a symphony as I race
on tiptoe towards the car to retrieve
grandpa's tackle box and fishing poles.

Arms flailing, all akimbo, he howls
a stream of laughter as the pair charge
after my slow-motion feet, retreating
with the pace of the summer sunshine.

I turn back
to see them fall,
plummeting
to the gravel;
she twists,
protecting our son,
and hits the ground,
hard.

She disappears beneath a sea of obscenities
as I rush to discover a trail of blood
cascading down his pained expression.

My shirt serves to stop the flow,
but he's ok, saved by his mother
who chose, in a moment,
to shield him from the blow

and earned in return,
as we will later learn
at the hospital, surgery
for a broken clavicle.

Written in Fire
6.26.20

What does your memory read
of the story we wrote that night?
Does the picture
on the canvas
of your mind,
paint the rebellion
and the might
our brushes burned
upon the stars
in our backyard?
Do the typewriter keys
clack in remembrance
of the fiery attack
we blazed to say
we'd had enough?
Or does that fire pit
inferno that we penned,
remind you
of two best friends,
who chose
to light a message
to each other
that simply said,
"Let's create together
until our art writes out its end."

Said the Air Part 2
6.28.20

You're at home
with your windows closed
to keep me out.

And I feel lonely.

I want to help
but it's true,
I'm the fight
you can't attack,
the sickness
you can't treat,
the very air
you fear to breathe.

I want to see you,
but more than that,
I want you to come back out.

Soothe a Burn
6.30.20

I was a blister
in the summer heat,
begging for
some sweet relief,
then you stepped in
with a lover's ease
and finally
brought the breeze.

Song of Extinction
7.1.20
   - In memory of Grant Berkland

Sifting through the colossal collection,
excavating the bones of burnt CDs
to find the fossils of reflection,
preserving a lifetime, left incomplete.

Brushing through the dirty decades,
selections of protected music taste
from the king of introspection,
now a skeleton kept safe

in a case of written labels
and messages known to him alone:

here rests the relic of an era,
a dinosaur compiled to be his own.

Safe in the Algorithm
7.3.20

This damn algorithm
keeps providing the same faces,
expressing similar views
and opinions. It's comforting
to collect and recognize
all the connections in our lives,
but is the point of society
to just consume?
Keep repeating the routine
to a constant, listening
group, supporting what you do?

Wouldn't it be better
to be met with opposition
and discover something new?

O Say Can You Hear?
7.4.20
   - To the tune of the Star-Spangled Banner

O say can you hear,
through the haze of this fight,
how loudly they wail
with the might of their dreaming?

Whose signs bear the scars
and the weight of a life
told by those kept in charge,
it pays to be white.

And the rocks of the scared,
thrown by those unaware,
are proof that Black lives
bear a tax we don't share.

O see how that blood-splattered
nation won't change
a policy born
on the backs of its slaves.

Calloused
7.7.20

A blemished mess of torn tissue
and disconnected skin reborn,
a ripped body of routine stains,
bleached and then stitched closed.

A collective mass of fragile flesh
that serves to dress the ghost
in permanent reminders of the depth
one cut can press into fresh hope.

A tattoo you didn't choose,
that blueprints where you've been,
the protection life selected
to speak for all you've hidden
in the safe space within the skin.

A callous is a wound
that grew to be a scar,
the imperfection you've accepted
as a part of who you are.

Seven Years Ago
7.8.20

Seven years ago,
you placed a pen
in the space we shared
while holding hands.
The ink became a color
you can't help but taste –
a flavor that grew into
a weird favorite –
and from this mixture
we drew together
our fabled pages,
creating domestic myths
to entertain the ages
we passed through.
Every letter since,
we sign with the kiss
of our sacred union
and seal with the promise
found in me and you.

Where's the Difference?
7.10.20

In 2011, Tanya McDowell,
a black woman,
living between a van
and a homeless shelter,
falsified her address
for the chance to send
her six-year-old son
to a better education.

In 2017, Felicity Huffman,
a white woman,
starring on television,
paid $15,000 to ensure
a new SAT score
and send her daughter,
of seventeen,
to an acting college.

Previous petty charges,
led Tanya McDowell
to take a plea deal
sentencing her
to five years
with no chance
for appeal.

Felicity Huffman's
record was blank
as white paper
and she received
fourteen days
(served eleven)
and a heavy fine
she easily paid.

Apparently, the comparison's unfair
because Tanya had been previously arrested.

But who fought to provide
for her child
in the smog of poverty
and only had time to barter with?

And who could afford
a slap on the wrist
and has a child currently enrolled
in the school she picked?

Both mothers lied to give their child
a shot at success.

So, before you disregard the comparison,
ponder the question:

Where's the difference?

Follow
7.13.20

Flip. Scroll. Glimpse. Link.
Like. Love. Swipe. Blink.

The arteries of our daily lives
corrode with each snapshot lie
we upload to social media,
blocking healthy honesty
with filtered photographs
that simplify
humanity's complexity
into easy-to-digest,
subscription packages.

Bite-size bits of data
entirely map a lifetime
and attract a community
of followers,
swallowing junk food captions,
written to salt the tastebuds
of the young and hungry,
infecting victims
with compliment-coded systems
created to feed
and addict.

It's an investment
for a platform to
capitalize on lives,
writing formulas
that cheaply twist
rich personalities
into contorted
character limits.

Smile. Move. Light. Switch.
Force. Hide. Craft. Fix.

Another soul sold for the price of a click.

Worth It
7.15.20

Two additional friends
and it's Christmas.
The libations poured,
the games, well chosen,
lay ignored on a table
boasting an array
of brightly colored feet.
It's been months
since we dared
proximity like this,
and as we laugh,
unmasked,
we're reminded
how good it feels
to bask
in joyful company.
It still feels irresponsible,
this small gathering
of estranged individuals,
but what are we living for
hiding from the ones
who make us smile?
Isn't a moment
of dangerous frivolity
worth the risk
once in a while?

A Mask Is
7.16.20

a symbol in America
representing freedoms
and the right to choose,
not designed to be used
as a tool promoting a political agenda.

to protect against a virus
that has killed 138,000 Americans
and 585,000 across the globe.
And that number will grow.

not created to ridicule,
not meant to split
or divide the nation
based on political parties.

a tool for safety
in this common Covid-fight
not a target for the selfish
who put lives behind their rights.

a silent love letter
that whispers boldly to the world,
"I am an individual,
I value certain things
but I don't deserve to freely speak
over the vulnerable souls
this breath could reach."

Open the Schools
7.20.20

The death toll's only increased
alongside the list
of what still remains unknown
about the Covid-19 virus.

An average classroom
at the high school level
will witness thirty different kids,
roughly every sixty minutes,
and CDC policy dictates
the exposed
must be quarantined
for two weeks
before allowed to return.

So how can educators
be expected
to maintain momentum
and create meaningful lessons,
when children
are continuously
forced to leave school?

If distance learning's inevitable,
why are we fighting the change?

I Exist for Us to Write
7.22.20

At twenty-four, in Iowa
I got my first tattoo
to commemorate the mantra
I wrote down at twenty-two.

Seven years have passed
and the ink begins to fade,
as I stare hard at my forearm
to remember why I saved

all the letters in this order,
sitting alone at UNI,
overflowing with creation
and an optimistic eye.

I know it was important,
this single written phrase,
but the poem to where it's scripted
has been overcome by age.

I want to write for others,
find the verses in their lives
but is that the only reason
I chose to carve this line

in the flesh upon my body,
for everyone to see
and constantly question
exactly what it means?

I am a storyteller,
by passion and by trade,
whether as a teacher
or a character on stage.

When I call myself a poet,
it's not about the rhymes,
I work to tell the story
in the pages of our times.

I observe the world around me
and notice how it moves,
I listen for the secrets
hidden underneath false truths.

I hear the cut of hatred,
and the gentle kiss of love,
the whispers of the voices
beneath our dying sun.

Every day I'm learning
who I will become,
I don't know where I'm going,
for I have just begun.

I do not have the wisdom,
nor do I have the right,
all I can do is listen
and exist for us to write.

Several poems in the collection have previously appeared or will appear in the following publications:

Grant's Goodbye *(originally titled 'Coma') – *Train River Publishing* (Summer Anthology)
Tiger King – *Train River Publishing* (Covid Anthology – forthcoming)
A Reminder – *Train River Publishing* (Covid Anthology – forthcoming)
A Reminder –*Wanderlust Books* (The Wanderlust Literary Journal)
Out Again *(originally titled 'Out') – *Train River Publishing* (Covid Anthology – forthcoming)
The Rockstar of America – *Train River Publishing* (Covid Anthology – forthcoming)
Dry Hands – *Poetry in the Time of Corona Virus* (The Anthology Vol. 2)
"Normal" – *Riza Press* (The Uncertain Creative)
If Walls Could Hear *(originally titled 'If Walls Could Talk') – *Festival for Poetry*

THANK YOU

to everyone who supported me on this journey. A big shout out to Brian Good for taking the time to help revise and format this collection—you're a good man. Also, to Vivian M. Cook and Taylor Sklenar, you're perspectives and insight were revelatory. To my wife, Meghan Kent, for allowing me the space and resources required to create this dream of a book. I would also like to thank my sisters, Alyssa and Kytana, and my mom and dad, Jerri and Chris, for their continued support and feedback. Thank you to Kivan Kirk and Avery Kent, two souls that push me to be better every day. A huge thank you to Brianne and Grant Berkland, whose stories I will continue to tell. To Ravastra Design Studio who took a concept and created something spectacular, your work ethic and dedication to this project was outstanding. Lastly, to all my friends and family, and anyone who happened to pass through my life, you are kidding yourself if you don't think a piece of you is here.
Thank you.

www.ingramcontent.com/pod-product-compliance
Lightning Source LLC
Chambersburg PA
CBHW031629040426
42452CB00007B/748